Contents

GW00818589

Introduction   **5**

Prácticas de pronunciación

Práctica 1   Pronunciation of 'ce', 'ci' and 'z'   11

Práctica 2   Pronunciation of 'b' and 'v'   12

Práctica 3   Vowels   14

Práctica 4   Pronunciation of diphthongs   15

Práctica 5   The sound /r/   17

Práctica 6   Pronunciation of 'd'   19

Práctica 7   The pronunciation of 'ge', 'gi' ' and 'j': [h] or [x]   20

Práctica 8   Pronunciation of 'g': /g/   21

Práctica 9   Stress in single words: 'agudas' and 'graves'   22

Práctica 10 Pronunciation of 'll' and 'y'   23

Práctica 11 Pronunciation of the letters 'p' and 't' and the sound /k/   24

Práctica 12 Stressed and unstressed vowels   26

Práctica 13 Intonation pattern of statements   27

Práctica 14 Pronunciation of 'h'   28

Práctica 15 Intonation pattern of yes/no questions   28

Práctica 16 Pronunciation of words that change meaning
             with shifts in stress   29

Práctica 17 The sound /rr/   30

Práctica 18 Pronunciation of the letter 'ñ'   32

Práctica 19 Pronunciation of the letter combination 'ch'   33

Práctica 20 Intonation patterns of content questions   34

Práctica 21 Vowels in contact: two-vowel synalepha   36

Práctica 22 Pronunciation of 'l'   37

Práctica 23 Stress in single words: 'esdrújulas' and 'sobresdrújulas'   38

Práctica 24 Hiatos   39

Práctica 25 Loss of stress in single phonic groups   39

Práctica 26 [δ] and [r] in intervocalic position   41

Práctica 27 Intonation pattern of exclamations   42

Práctica 28 Intonation pattern of multiple phonic groups: enumerations 43

Práctica 29 Stress in compound nouns   44

Práctica 30 Combinations of consonants   44

Práctica 31 Assimilation of consonants   45

Práctica 32 Pronunciation of words with two stresses:
             adverbs ending in '-mente'   45

Práctica 33 Pronunciation of 'x'   46

Práctica 34 Intonation pattern of imperative sentences   46

Práctica 35 Intonation patterns of sentences with multiple
             phonic groups: parenthetic phrases   48

Práctica 36 Pronunciation of long words: verb forms with enclitics   48

Práctica 37 Triphthongs and three-vowel synalepha   49

Práctica 38 Intonation pattern of disjunctive sentences   50

Práctica 39 Integrated activity   51

Clave   **52**

Introduction

Welcome to the *En rumbo* pronunciation activities! This booklet and the accompanying audio cassettes are intended to improve your speaking and listening skills by practising the sounds, rhythm and intonation of spoken Spanish. They can be used in conjunction with the Spanish course *En rumbo* or on their own for whatever reason (if you feel speaking is your weakest skill, or you have an oral exam or a trip to a Spanish-speaking country impending, for example).

The Pronunciation Practice Cassettes feature speakers from different regions of the Spanish-speaking world, in order to familiarize you with a variety of Spanish accents. As you practise speaking, you should try to adopt either a Castilian or a non-Castilian pronunciation (see below), according to which is more useful or easier for you. Neither of these varieties is more 'correct' than the other. Whichever pronunciation you choose, you should try to be consistent. The terms 'Castilian' and 'non-Castilian' are broad generalizations which refer to the pronunciation of certain sounds in central and northern Spain (Castilian) and the rest of Spain, the Canary Islands and the Spanish-speaking Americas (non-Castilian):

- the 'c' in 'ce' and 'ci' and 'z' are pronounced like the 'th' in English 'thin' in Castilian Spanish and like the 's' in English 'soft' in non-Castilian Spanish.

- the 'g' in 'ge' and 'gi' and 'j' are pronounced like the 'ch' in Scottish 'loch' in Castilian Spanish and like the 'h' in English 'he' in non-Castilian Spanish.

The cassettes contain extracts of natural spoken Spanish, in order to expose you to the way native speakers of Spanish speak and the sort of Spanish you are likely to hear.

Spanish is said to be an 'easy language to learn badly'. Because Spanish has a simpler sound structure than English or French, and because its spelling is highly phonetic, it gives the impression that it can be learned with little practice. This is not the case. The reason for the activities in this booklet is precisely to give you additional opportunities to practise spoken Spanish and to 'learn it well'.

Reference will be made to the parts of the mouth and throat used to speak and particular ways they are used to produce the Spanish sounds, especially those sounds that do not exist in English.

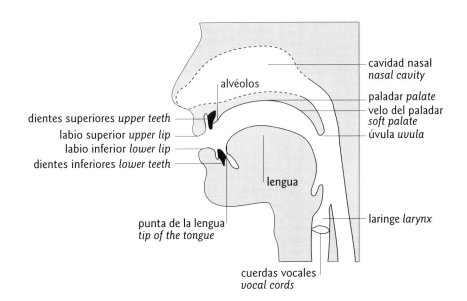

Symbols

We will use the following symbols where appropriate to represent the Spanish sounds:

Vowel sounds

/ɑ/ as the 'a' in 'apple'.

/e/ as the 'e' in 'pen'.

/i/ as the 'ea' in 'seat'.

/o/ as the 'o' in 'dot'.

/u/ as the 'oo' in 'boot'.

Consonant sounds

[b] as the 'b' in 'book'. It is represented in written Spanish by the letters 'b' and 'v'. It occurs after a pause or 'm' or 'n'.

[β] soft bilabial sound pronounced like a [b], but with the lips close rather than touching. It is represented in written Spanish by the letters 'b' and 'v' and occurs between vowels.

[d] as the 'd' in 'den'. It is represented in written Spanish by the letter 'd' and it occurs after a pause or after 'n' or 'l'.

[ð] as the 'th' of 'that'. It is represented in written Spanish by the letter 'd' and occurs between vowels.

/f/ as the 'f' in 'feet'.

/g/ as the 'g' in 'get'. It is represented in written Spanish by 'gu' when followed by 'e' or 'i' (where the 'u' is silent) and by the letter 'g' in the combinations 'ga', 'go', 'gu', 'güe' and 'güi'.

/ʝ/ like the 'y' in 'yet' in Spain or the 'J' in 'John' in parts of Spain and Spanish America. It is represented in written Spanish by 'll' or 'y'.

/k/ as the 'c' in 'cap', but without the exhaled air that accompanies the equivalent sound in English. It is represented in Spanish by 'qu' when followed by 'e' or 'i' (where the 'u' is silent) and the letter 'c' in the combinations 'ca', 'co' and 'cu'.

/l/ as the 'l' in 'lid'.

/m/ as the 'm' in 'most'.

/n/ as the 'n' in 'not'.

/ɲ/ as the 'ni' of 'onion' and the 'gn' in 'lasagne'.

/p/ as the 'p' in 'spin'.

/r/ as the 'tt' in US English 'pretty' or 'better'.

/rr/ as the rolled 'r' found in some Scottish dialects.

/s/ as the 's' in 'stop'.

/θ/ as the 'th' in 'thin'.

/t/ as the 't' in 'step'.

/tʃ/ as the 'ch' in 'church'.

[ɦ] as the 'h' in 'he'.

[x] as the 'ch' in Scottish 'loch' or German 'auch'.

Reference will also be made to the Spanish alphabet and how each letter is pronounced. We use signs for phonemes (see page 10), which are within slashes e.g. /a/, and allophones, which appear within square brackets, e.g. [β].

Letter	Name
a	a
b	be /be/ *or* be larga (Spanish America)
c	ce /se/ *or* /θe/
d	de /de/
e	e
f	efe /efe/
g	ge [he] *or* [xe]
h	hache /atʃe/
i	i
j	jota [hota] *or* [xota]
k	ka
l	ele
m	eme
n	ene
ñ	eñe
o	o
p	pe
q	cu
r	erre *or* ere (Spanish America)
s	ese
t	te
u	u
v	uve (Spain) *or* be corta *or* be chiquita (Spanish America)
w	uve doble (Spain) *or* doble u (Spanish America)
x	equis
y	i griega (Spain) *or* ye (Spanish America)
z	zeta /seta/ *or* /θeta/

The stress mark

In order to show which syllable of a word carries the major stress in phonetic transcription the character ' is used before the stressed syllable. For example, in /espaˈɲol/, the syllable '-ñol' in the word *español* is stressed.

Glossary

We make use of the following terms in these materials.

acento ortográfico / tilde   the acute accent used to mark the stressed syllable in some Spanish words, e.g. *bebé, acción, ángel, teléfono.*

agudas   words that carry their stress on the last syllable, e.g. *amor, canción, papá.*

allophone   form of a phoneme, e.g. the [δ] of *nada* and the [d] of *doctor.*

alveolar   describes a sound produced by touching the alveoli (upper gums) with the tip of the tongue, e.g. English /d/.

alveoli   the tooth ridges (gums).

aspiration   puff of air that accompanies the English sounds /p/, /t/ and /k/ in initial position.

atonic   describes a vowel that does not carry stress, e.g. the 'a' in 'activity'.

bilabial   a sound produced with both the upper and the lower lip, e.g. the /b/ of *boca,* the /p/ of *punto* and the /m/ of *mucho.*

dental   describes a sound produced by touching the back of the upper teeth with the tip of the tongue, e.g. /n/.

diaeresis   mark over a 'u' that shows that the 'u' is pronounced, e.g. *lingüística.*

diphthong   the combination of /i/ or /u/ with any other vowel sound or with each other, e.g. *ciudad, cuidado, hay, oiga.*

disjunctive sentence   a sentence made up of phrases or other sentences joined by *o* or *u*, e.g. *Teresa no entiende o no tiene interés.*

esdrújulas   words that carry their stress on the third syllable from the end, e.g. *último, buenísimo, esdrújula.*

graves   words that carry their stress on the penultimate syllable, e.g. *casa, universo, cárcel.*

homophones   words which are pronounced the same, e.g. *vota* and *bota* are both pronounced /bota/.

intervocalic   describes a sound that occurs between two vowels, e.g. the first 'b' in 'rhubarb'.

intonation contour   lines used to show intonation patterns.

labiodental describes a sound pronounced by touching the lower lip with the upper teeth, e.g. /f/.

palatal describes a sound produced by touching the palate with the middle part of the tongue, e.g. /tʃ/.

phoneme a speech sound.

phonic group a group of sounds uttered between two pauses.

sobresdrújulas words that carry their stress on the fourth syllable from the end, e.g. *cuéntamelas, cuídateme, prométemelo.*

stress the extra emphasis put on one or more syllables when pronouncing a word, e.g. in the word 'constitution' the stress falls on 'tu'.

syllable-final sound at the end of a syllable, e.g. the /s/ in *vis-ta.*

synalepha the elision of syllables that occurs when a word ends in a vowel and the next word begins with a vowel sound, e.g. in *mi hermana* the syllables /mi/ and /er/ become the single syllable /mier/.

tonic describes a stressed vowel, e.g. the first 'i' in 'activity'.

triphthong combination of three vowels: /uai/, /uei/, /iai/, /iei/, e.g. *guay, buey.*

velar a sound pronounced by touching the soft palate (velum) with the back of the tongue, e.g. the /g/ of *gordo* or the /k/ of *kilo.*

Now over to you. Enjoy it!

Prácticas de pronunciación

Práctica 1 Pronunciation of 'ce', 'ci' and 'z'

Remember that the 'c' in 'ce' and 'ci' and the letter 'z' are pronounced /θ/ by Castilian speakers and /s/ by non-Castilian speakers. You therefore have a choice of pronunciation of these letter combinations. If you are going to adopt a Castilian pronunciation you should do *Ejercicio 1*, otherwise concentrate on *Ejercicio 2*.

Ejercicio 1 | Listen to the following words pronounced by a Castilian speaker:

> nací, centro, Galicia, luz, Cuzco

Ejercicio 2 | Now listen to a non-Castilian speaker.

> nací, centro, Galicia, luz, Cuzco

Ejercicio 3 | Listen to the following pairs of words. The words in each pair have different meanings. Remember that non-Castilian speakers do not differentiate between /s/ and /θ/: to them these pairs of words are homophones, i.e. they sound the same.

poso I pose	*pozo* well
as ace	*haz* do
asar grill	*azar* chance
casa house	*caza* hunt
coser to sew	*cocer* to cook

This does not normally cause confusion as the context clarifies any possible ambiguities. In some cases, alternative words have evolved, such as *cacería* (for *caza*) and *cocinar* (for *cocer*).

Ejercicio 4 | Listen to the following two extracts and decide whether each person is speaking with a Castilian or a non-Castilian pronunciation:

(a) Aparte de eso tiene un poco de todo. Tiene mar, montaña. Eh… no es muy grande ni muy pequeña la ciudad. Tiene unas avenidas muy bonitas. También hay que decir que tiene unos barrios marginales bastante deprimidos. En fin, que tenemos de todo.

(b) Dicen que el danzón se baila en un cuadrito, porque la gente no se desplaza mucho. Dicen que la pareja que sabe bailar bien bien el danzón, te baila arriba de un mosaico, por lo tan pegadito que está la pareja, ¿no? Ahí dicen que ahí se enamoraban antes las parejas, bailando danzón. Y esas parejas que se enamoraban bailando danzón te aseguro que son esos viejitos que todavía siguen yendo a bailar danzón.

Ejercicio 5

Read the transcript of the extracts in *Ejercicio 4* aloud. Decide beforehand if you are going to use /s/ throughout or a combination of /s/ and /θ/ as appropriate. However, you must try to be consistent!

Ejercicio 6

Listen to the following riddle. First you will hear a Castilian speaker, then a non-Castilian one read it. Choose the version that suits you better, then rewind the cassette and shadow read it. Remember to be consistent in your choice of pronunciation.

Es grandote, muy panzón
y con jamón se utiliza;
al que nace cabezón
su cabeza así bautizan.

(Schujer, Silvia, *350 adivinanzas para jugar,* 1995, p. 20)

The answer to the riddle is in the *Clave*.

Práctica 2 Pronunciation of 'b' and 'v'

In Spanish, the letters 'b' and 'v' are pronounced the same.

Ejercicio 7

Listen to the words and repeat after each pair:

vamos	barrio
Venus	Begoña
viejito	bigote
voy	boca

There are two variants of the sound represented by the letters 'b' and 'v': [β], the most frequent, occurs in intervocalic position (*Isabel, oveja*), and is pronounced with the lips slightly open, rather like when you gently blow out a match. To the Anglophone ear it often sounds like an English 'v', but make sure you do not pronounce it as such. The second variant, [b] occurs after a pause or after 'm' or 'n' (*embarazo, convento*) and it sounds very much like the English 'b' in 'berry' or 'book'.

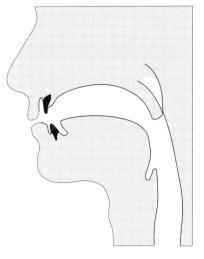

Articulación de [β]

Ejercicio 8

Listen to the contrast between the two variants of 'b'.

vida	esta vida
bien	¡Qué bien!
Villarrica	de Villarrica
Buga	a Buga

Ejercicio 9

Listen to the following extract, and on the transcript below mark the places where the two variants [b] and [β] occur. Then read the extract aloud.

En ese instante, las dos mujeres ven llegar a través de la ventana a Carlos y Zacarías. Bajan entonces a la calle para recibirlos.

Rosita   ¡Abuelo!

Zacarías   ¡Rosita, mi niña! ¡Qué ganas tenía de verte! Pero a ver, déjame que te vea. ¡Si estás más alta!

Rosita   ¡Anda, abuelo! ¡Si me ves cada mes! No seas exagerado.

Isabel   Hola, don Zacarías. ¿Cómo le fue en el viaje?

Zacarías   Hola, Isabel. ¿El viaje? Bien, bien. Lo peor ha sido de la estación hasta aquí. ¡Cómo está Madrid! ¡Mucho coche y mucho humo! ¡Y todo el mundo con prisas! No sé yo si me voy a acostumbrar a esta vida de ciudad.

Carlos   Papá, no empieces con lo de siempre. Aquí estarás perfectamente bien.

Rosita   Abuelo, esto te va a gustar mucho. En algunas cosas es peor que el pueblo, pero en otras es mejor. Madrid tiene cantidad de cosas interesantes. Ya verás.

Cinta 1   Cara A

Carlos   Bueno, ya está bien de saludos. Ahora subamos todas estas maletas.

Isabel   Pero, don Zacarías, ¿dónde vamos a meter todo esto en el apartamento? ¿Seguro que lo necesita todo?

Zacarías   Claro que sí.

Rosita   Venga, abuelo, subamos. Deja que te lleve esa maleta tan grandota, que desde que hago pesas estoy hecha una cachas.

Zacarías   No, Rosita, ésta la llevo yo.

Ejercicio 10

Listen to the pronunciation of 'b' and 'v' in the following riddle. Then read the riddle aloud.

A veces rugiendo
a veces silbando
nadie me ha visto
que paso volando
A veces rugiendo
a veces silbando
nadie me mira, cuando voy pasando.

(Schujer, Silvia, *350 adivinanzas para jugar,* 1995, p. 72)

Práctica 3 Vowels

There are only five vowel sounds in Spanish: /a/, /e/, /i/, /o/ and /u/, which are pronounced approximately as in English **a**pple, **e**cho, b**ea**t, **o**ff and b**oo**t. They are clear, short and clipped. The quality of these sounds varies little with the surrounding sounds, their position in a word, or stress. When any of these vowels appear at the end of a syllable, English speakers must avoid 'opening' them; thus words like *que* and *solo* must not be pronounced like the English 'Kay' and 'solo'. Also, the 'e' in final, unstressed position is never silent, as in /importante/.

Ejercicio 11

Listen to the following words and repeat after each word.

/a/	/e/	/i/	/o/	/u/
casa	dentro	miles	cómo	Coruña
España	México	bonita	millón	lluvia
Málaga	época	fin	boca	Cataluña
está	bebé	niño	bigote	Perú
antes	cabello	Lalín	ocho	mucho

14

Ejercicio 12	Listen to the cassette and notice the difference between /e/ and /i/. Repeat after each pair of words.

/e/	/i/
mesa	misa
queso	quiso
beso	viso
peso	piso
case	casi

Ejercicio 13	Listen to the following words. Concentrate on the /e/ and /o/ sounds at the end of each word and repeat.

/e/	/o/
sé	pero
equipaje	bonito
habitante	puerto
sobresaliente	México

Ejercicio 14

Listen for the vowel sounds in the following rhyme.

> Salió la 'a', no sé a dónde va.
> Fue a comprarle un regalo a su mamá.
>
> Salió la 'e', no sé a dónde fue.
> Fue con su tía Marta a tomar té.
>
> Salió la 'i', y yo no la sentí.
> Fue a comprar un puntico para mí.
>
> Salió la 'o', y casi no volvió.
> Se fue a comer tamales y se engordó.
>
> Salió la 'u', y qué me dices tú.
> Se fue en su bicicleta y llegó al Perú.

puntico
dot on the 'i'

tamal
ound maize with meat
sweet filling wrapped
in a banana leaf

Práctica 4 Pronunciation of diphthongs

When two vowels come together in the same syllable within a word they form a sound combination known as a diphthong, for example: *bueno, nieve, aire*.

Cinta 1 Cara A

15

There are fourteen diphthongs in Spanish and they are the result of the combination of 'i' and 'u' with the other vowels and with each other.

ia	ie	io	iu
ai	ei	oi	ui
ua	ue	uo	
au	eu	ou	

Ejercicio 15

Listen to the following examples of the fourteen diphthongs:

ia	familia	**eu**	seudónimo
ai, **ay**	aire, caray	**io**	periódico
ua	agua	**oi**, **oy**	boina
au	fauna	**uo**	antiguo
ie	quien	**ou**	COU
ei, **ey**	veinte, ley	**iu**	diurno
ue	encuentra	**ui**, **uy**	ruinas, muy

Ejercicio 16

Listen to the following passage and mark the diphthongs in the transcript below.

Empezamos diariamente a las siete treinta recibiendo la guardia de las últimas veinticuatro horas. A las ocho pasamos a las salas a ver los pacientes que han ingresado, eh… de una manera rápida. En una hora revisamos los ingresos. De las nueve a las once, paso visita en alguna de las salas específicas, eh… rotándolas. De once a doce tenemos alguna reunión, algún tipo de sesión también presentada por algún servicio. A las doce tenemos actividades… del comité de calidad, o bien… eh, de actividad general del hospital. A partir de las dos de la tarde nos dedicamos a labores docentes, educativas hasta las catorce o… hasta las dieciséis o diecisiete horas.

Ejercicio 17

Listen to the following poem by the Chilean poet, Gabriela Mistral. Mark the diphthongs and then read the poem aloud:

Nocturno

Padre nuestro, que estás en los cielos,
¿por qué te has olvidado de mí?
Te acordaste del fruto en febrero,
al llegarse su pulpa rubí.
¡Llevo abierto también mi costado
y no quieres mirar hacia mí!

Me vendió el que besó mi mejilla;
me negó por la túnica ruin.
Yo en mis versos el rostro con sangre,
como Tú sobre el paño, le di;
y en mi noche del Huerto me han sido,
Juan cobarde, y el Ángel hostil.

(*Los 25.000 mejores versos de la lengua castellana*, 1969, p. 391)

The first two lines of the poem are repeated on the cassette.

Práctica 5 The sound /ɾ/

The letter 'r' represents the Spanish sound /ɾ/ as in the word *aro* when it occurs in intervocalic position within a word *(verano)* and at the end of a syllable *(Guillermo, por)*. It is pronounced with a simple flap of the tongue against the upper gums like in US English 'da**dd**y', 'pre**tt**y' or 'be**tt**er'.

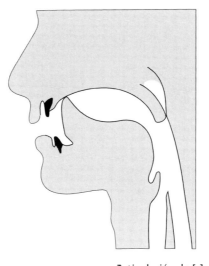

Articulación de [ɾ]

Ejercicio 18

Listen to the words and repeat after the tone:

colores, maravilla, caro, iremos

Ejercicio 19

Listen to the words and repeat after the tone. Make sure you pronounce the /ɾ/ sound distinctly.

mar, tirarse, divertido, deportes

Cinta 1 Cara A

The /r/ sound at the end of a syllable, especially at the end of a word, needs to be pronounced clearly to avoid any confusion.

Ejercicio 20

Listen to the following pairs of words and repeat them after the tone.

caló language of Spanish gypsies	*calor* heat
amó loved	*amor* love
bebé baby	*beber* to drink
tembló shook	*temblor* tremor

The /r/ sound characterizes the Spanish infinitive. It is very important to pronounce this sound in the infinitive endings.

Ejercicio 21

Listen to the following words and for each, add /r/ after the tone to form an infinitive, as in the example.

Ejemplo

salí   salir

está

oí

salí

así

Ejercicio 22

The /r/ sound also characterizes the simple future tense in Spanish. Listen to the following sentences in the present tense and convert them to sentences in the future, as in the example:

Ejemplo

Nos juntamos un grupo de amigos.
Nos juntaremos un grupo de amigos.

Preparamos el material necesario.

Viajamos en coche.

Nos comemos una buena comida.

Ejercicio 23

Listen for the /r/ sound in the following rhyme by the Spanish poet Federico García Lorca, then rewind the cassette and listen to it line by line.

Mariposa del aire, qué hermosa eres,
mariposa del aire dorada y verde.
No te quieres parar, pararte no quieres.
Mariposa del aire dorada y verde.

(Jiménez, Juan Ramón *et al*, *Mi primer libro de poemas,* 1997, p. 67)

Cinta 1   Cara A

Práctica 6 Pronunciation of 'd'

In Spanish, the letter 'd' is pronounced in two different ways according to where it appears in a word or phrase. [δ], the most frequent, occurs in intervocalic position (*todas, me dices*), before and after 'r' (*tarde, padre*) and at the end of syllables (*admitir, salud*). It is very close to the English 'th' in 'this' or 'though'. The other pronunciation [d] occurs after a pause, after 'n' (*donde*) or 'l' (*Matilde*), and is pronounced in a similar way to the English 'd' in 'den', but with the tip of the tongue touching the back of the upper teeth rather than the gums.

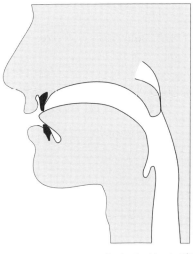

Articulación de [ð]

Ejercicio 24

Listen for the sound [δ] in the following words and repeat after the tone. Remember that this sound occurs when 'd' appears in intervocalic position, either within a word like in *llegada* or across word boundaries as in *quiero decir*.

planeado, escalada, comida, todo

Ejercicio 25

Listen to the following words containing the sound [d] and repeat after the tone. Remember that [d] is pronounced with the tip of the tongue touching the upper teeth.

deporte, domingo, donde, cuando

Ejercicio 26

Listen for the contrast between the two pronunciations of the letter 'd'.

dama	una dama
desastre	otro desastre
dura	qué dura
derecho	no hay derecho

Ejercicio 27

Listen for occurrences of the two pronunciations of the letter 'd' in the following extract. Mark the places where each of them occurs in the transcript below, then read the extract aloud.

> Pocos días después de su llegada, Zacarías sigue adaptándose a la vida de la gran ciudad. Ha visitado ya el club de jubilados del barrio y se ha apuntado a una de sus actividades: un campeonato de damas, un juego de mesa que le gusta mucho.
>
> Es por la tarde. Carlos y Zacarías juegan a las damas en el salón de su casa. Están también presentes Isabel, que cose, y Rosita, que lee un libro.
>
> **Zacarías** ¡Vamos, Carlos, no te distraigas tanto! ¡Que estamos jugando en serio!
>
> **Carlos** Bueno, papá, no te lo tomes así. Es sólo un juego.
>
> **Zacarías** Sí, pero no puedes estar todo el tiempo mirando a todos lados menos al tablero.
>
> **Carlos** Es que tú tardas mucho en mover las fichas.

When 'd' appears at the end of a word or phrase, as in the word *universidad*, it is normally pronounced [ð]: [uniβersi'ðað], although it can also be pronounced [θ]: [uniβersi'ðaθ] by Castilian speakers or not pronounced at all by speakers from any region [uniβersi'ða].

Ejercicio 28

Listen for the pronunciation of the letter 'd' in the following lines by the Spanish mystic poet, Fray Luis de León. Rewind the cassette, listen to the poem a second time and shadow read it.

> ¡Qué descansada vida
> la del que huye del mundanal ruido
> y sigue la escondida
> senda por donde han ido
> los pocos sabios que en el mundo han sido!

(*Los 25.000 mejores versos de la lengua castellana*, 1969, p. 86)

Práctica 7 The pronunciation of 'ge', 'gi' and 'j': [h] or [x]

In Spanish, the letter 'g' in the combinations 'ge' and 'gi' and the letter 'j' are pronounced like the 'h' of English 'he'. Some Castilian speakers pronounce it [x], like the 'ch' of Scottish 'loch'. Neither pronunciation is more 'correct' than the other.

Ejercicio 29	Listen to the words and notice the two sounds, [h] and [x]. Decide which pronunciation suits you better and repeat each word.

> surgir, gente, bajaremos, abajo

Ejercicio 30	Listen to the following English words and give the Spanish for each one, after the tone. The Spanish words must contain the sound [h] or [x]. Choose the pronunciation that suits you better.

> ham, game, jug, people

Ejercicio 31	Listen for the pronunciation of 'ge', 'gi' and the letter 'j' in the following rhyme, read first by a non-Castilian speaker and then by a Castilian. Choose the pronunciation that suits you better and read the rhyme aloud.

> Gisela, Juana y Gerardo,
> junto con Jorge y Jesús
> van a Fuengirola en jaca,
> pero nunca en autobús.

jaca
small horse

Práctica 8 Pronunciation of 'g': /g/

In Spanish, the letter 'g' in the letter combinations 'ga', 'go' and 'gu' is pronounced like the 'g' of English 'get'.

Ejercicio 32	Listen to the words and repeat after the tone.

> ganar, tengo, segundo, gorro

In the letter combinations 'gue' and 'gui' the 'u' is silent, as in English 'guitar'.

Ejercicio 33	Listen to the words and repeat after the tone.

> higuera, guerra, merengue, Guillermo

In the letter combinations 'güe' and 'güi', the diaeresis over the 'u' indicates that the 'u' must be pronounced. These letter combinations are pronounced like English 'penguin' and 'unguent'.

Ejercicio 34	Listen to the words and repeat after the tone.

> bilingüe, pingüino, lingüista, piragüismo

Ejercicio 35

Listen to the contrast between /g/ and /h/; after the tone read each pair of words aloud.

paga pays	*paja* straw
liguero suspender belt	*ligero* light, lightweight
águila eagle	*ágil* agile
gusto delight, taste	*justo* just, fair
hogueras bonfires	*ojeras* rings under the eyes

Ejercicio 36

Listen for the pronunciation of 'g' in the following tongue-twister. Listen to it in full first and then rewind the cassette and repeat after each line.

Un aguerrido guisante
guardaba un güero en Güimar,
cuando un guerrero bilingüe
guisando, salió a guerrear.

Práctica 9 Stress in single words: 'agudas' and 'graves'

Note that in the sentence '**Which** is the **bus** for **Ryde**, **please**?':

- there are four stressed syllables, shown in bold;
- 'Which' is separated from 'bus' by two unstressed syllables;
- 'bus' is separated from 'Ryde' by just one syllable;
- 'Ryde' and 'please' are not separated by any.

Because there is the same time interval between stressed syllables, unstressed syllables have to be spoken at variable speed and as a consequence they are often 'squashed'.

In the Spanish sentence *Quien mal **an**da mal a**ca**ba,* although there are two main stresses on the syllables 'an' of *anda* and 'ca' of *acaba*, all the syllables are roughly equal in length and no sound is neutralized or 'squashed'. In other words, in Spanish each syllable has to be uttered without changing the pronunciation of or swallowing unstressed syllables.

This rule applies equally to single words, where each syllable has to be pronounced in full. For instance, the word *maravilla* has four syllables, each of which must be spoken fully and in roughly the same amount of time: *ma-ra-vi-lla.* In addition, each letter 'a' is pronounced roughly the same.

Ejercicio 37 | Listen to the following words and repeat after the tone.

elefante, aficionado, temporada, demasiadas

Ejercicio 38 | Read the following sentences after the tone.

– Ha sido una sensación muy bonita.

– Sin duda alguna en el verano.

– No pasa nada si pierdo.

– ¿Has ido por fin al médico?

In most Spanish words, the main stress falls on just one syllable. You can tell where the stress is from the word ending. Here, we look at two types of word:

• those where the stress falls on the last syllable (*agudas*);

• those where it falls on the penultimate syllable (*graves* or *llanas*).

In order to determine where a word is stressed in Spanish, first check if there is a written accent on a vowel, as in *comeré*, *sábado* or *jamón*. If there is not, you need to look at its ending:

(a) If the word ends in 'd', 'j', 'l', 'm', 'r' or 'z', the stress falls on the last syllable, for example *ciudad*, *reloj*, *papel*, *amor*, *Veracruz*. These words are called *agudas*.

(b) If the word ends in a vowel, 'n' or 's', the stress falls on the penultimate syllable, for example *llegada*, *deporte*, *casi*, *alpinismo*, *tribu*, *olores*, *reparten*. These words are called *graves* or *llanas*.

Words like *está*, *bebé*, *aquí*, *pasó*, *nación* and *después*, *césped*, *árbol*, *álbum*, *alcázar* and *lápiz* have a written accent on the stressed vowel; they do not follow either of the rules above.

Ejercicio 39 | Listen to the following words and say *uno* if it is *aguda* or *dos* if it is *grave*. The answers are on the cassette.

Bogotá, jugar, jamás, piñata, fútbol

Práctica 10 Pronunciation of 'll' and 'y'

In Spanish 'll' and 'y' are pronounced the same. There are two main pronunciations: like the 'y' in English 'yes' or like the 'J' of 'John'. You therefore have a choice of pronunciation. It does not matter which you choose, as long as you are consistent with your earlier choice of pronunciation.

At the end of a word, 'y' always forms part of a diphthong or triphthong and is pronounced as the Spanish vowel 'i': *voy, hay, guay*. The Spanish word *y* ('and') is also pronounced /i/.

Cinta 1 Cara B

Some Spanish speakers in Castile and parts of Peru and Bolivia have kept the old pronunciation of 'll', similar to the English 'lli' of million but this Spanish sound is rapidly dying out.

Ejercicio 40

Listen to the words and repeat after the tone.

estrella, allí, oye, yo

Ejercicio 41

Listen to the words on the cassette and write them down or spell them in your head. Remember that at the end of a word, 'y' is pronounced as an 'i'.

Ejercicio 42

Listen to the following proverbs and repeat them after the tone.

Hasta el cuarenta de mayo, no te quites el sayo.

Mientras las armas hablan, las leyes callan.

El asno chiquillo siempre es borriquillo.

Now look up their English equivalents in the *Clave*.

Práctica 11 Pronunciation of the letters 'p' and 't' and the sound /k/

In Spanish the sounds /p/, /t/ and /k/ are pronounced without aspiration. They sound more like the 'p', 't' and 'k' of English s**p**in, s**t**and and s**k**i. Try pronouncing the English words 'pat', 'cake' and 'key' with a sheet of paper close to your mouth; you should notice that your breath as you pronounce the initial letters (aspiration) moves the paper. Now try pronouncing 'spin', 'stand' and 'ski'. You should notice that the paper does not move this time. This is how the Spanish sounds /p/, /t/ and /k/ are pronounced. The /p/ and /k/ are very similar to English, but the Spanish /t/ sound is dental rather than alveolar. When pronouncing /t/, the tip of the tongue must touch the back of the upper teeth, unlike in English, where it touches the upper gums.

Ejercicio 43

Listen to the words and repeat after the tone.

papá, profesional, piñata, político

Ejercicio 44

Listen to the following pairs of words and notice the difference between /p/ and /b/. Repeat after the tone.

pasado past	*basado* based
pelo hair	*velo* veil
piña pineapple	*viña* vineyard
pista clue, piste	*vista* view

Ejercicio 45

Listen for the pronunciation of the letter 'p' in the tongue-twister; then rewind the cassette and repeat it one line at a time. Remember that the Spanish /p/ has no aspiration.

> Paco Peco, chico rico
> insultaba como un loco a su tío Federico.
> Y éste dijo: 'Poco a poco, Paco Peco, poco pico'.

Ejercicio 46

Listen to the following words and repeat after the tone. Remember that the Spanish /t/ is dental and is not aspirated.

> tratamiento, tú, tecnología, también

Ejercicio 47

Listen to the following pairs of words and notice the difference between /t/ and /d/. Repeat after the tone.

te	de		tos	dos
tía	día		hada	ata

Ejercicio 48

Listen for the pronunciation of the letter 't' in the following proverbs; repeat each proverb during the gap. Remember that the Spanish /t/ is not aspirated and is a dental sound.

> A tales tiempos, tales alientos.
>
> Donde no hay mata, no hay patata.
>
> De tal palo, tal astilla.

Ejercicio 49

Listen to the words and repeat after the tone. Remember that the Spanish /k/ is not aspirated and that it is represented in written Spanish by 'c' or 'qu' in the following letter combinations: 'ca', 'co', 'cu', 'que', 'qui' and 'k'. Note that 'k' is only used in a few words of foreign origin, e.g. *kilómetro*.

> complejo, curar, ¿qué?, ¿quién?

Ejercicio 50

Listen to the following pairs of words and notice the difference between /k/ and /g/. Repeat after the tone.

col cabbage	*gol* goal (football)
coma comma	*goma* rubber
esta cuita this pain	*esta agüita* this drink of water (when talking to a small child)
quiso s/he wanted	*guiso* stew

Cinta 1 Cara B

Ejercicio 51 | Listen for the pronunciation of /k/ in the following tongue-twister; then rewind the cassette and repeat it line by line. You may also want to shadow read it the second time. Remember that the Spanish /k/ is not aspirated.

> Compadre, cómpreme un coco.
> Compadre, no compro coco.
> Porque como poco coco como,
> poco coco compro.

Ejercicio 52 | Listen to the following passage about alternative medicine paying special attention to the sounds /p/, /t/ and /k/. Mark on the text below the places where they occur and then read the text aloud.

> Tenemos desde luego que reconocer: la medicina naturista carece de todos los elementos políticos que nos hacen resentir hasta cierto punto a la medicina… vamos a decir 'de patente' o a la medicina soportada por investigación científica. Hay mucho discurso político alrededor de esto, a la gente se le hace sentir mal porque se le dice que es excesivamente cara. En muchos casos efectivamente lo es, pero yo te diría que en prácticamente todos esos casos lo es con justa razón. Lo que hay detrás de esa medicina poca gente lo conoce pero el hecho es que gracias a la investigación privada y al cuidado que se ha puesto, el promedio de vida del ser humano se ha incrementado notablemente.

Práctica 12 Stressed and unstressed vowels

Spanish vowels change very little when stressed. The change is in the vowel duration rather than sound quality. In the word *garganta*, for instance, the 'a' in 'gar' and 'ta' is slightly shorter than that in 'gan' which is stressed. Apart from that, the 'a' sound is no different. Unstressed vowels in Spanish do not change, unlike in English (notice, for instance, the difference in pronunciation of the second 'a' in the words 'analysis' and 'analyse').

Ejercicio 53 | Listen to the following words and repeat after the tone. Compare the duration of the stressed vowel with that of the unstressed vowel.

> espalda, enfermo, estómago, aspirina

Some Spanish words differ from others only in that one is stressed and another is unstressed. The stressed vowel is distinguished by a written accent.

Ejercicio 54

Listen to the following pairs of phrases and repeat after the tone. Compare the stressed version with the unstressed.

él bebe	**el** bebé
para **mí**	**mi** espalda
tú toses	**tu** tos
sé mucho	**se** vende

Práctica 13 Intonation pattern of statements

Statements are characterized by an intonation contour which rises on the first stressed syllable and stays the same until the last stressed syllable, where it falls below the initial pitch, as in the example.

Ejemplo

Mi trabajo es encargado de personal.

Although this intonation pattern applies to all statements, the contour between the first and the last stressed syllables is not always a straight, sustained one, but it depends on the number of syllables in between and on the sentence structure. This means that there are various contour patterns (which you will work on later). In this *Práctica*, we are dealing with sentences containing a single phonic group.

Ejercicio 55

Listen to these statements and follow the intonation pattern by shadow reading them.

– Me duele la espalda.

– Para olvidarme un poco de los problemas cotidianos.

– Tiene problemas de memoria.

– Eso al que tiene cólico se le da.

Ejercicio 56

Complete the following statements using the words in brackets, as in the example. Say the complete sentence after the tone.

Ejemplo

Aquí hace mucho… (calor)   Aquí hace mucho calor.

Me gusta más la… (medicina natural).

Se toma con agua caliente y… (miel).

Tengo que hacerme un… (análisis).

Ejercicio 57

Give short answers to the following questions using the words or expressions given as a prompt, as in the example.

Ejemplo

¿Qué tomas para el resfriado? (jarabe)   Tomo jarabe.

¿Cree en la medicina natural o en la convencional? (la natural)

¿Con qué frecuencia va al dentista? (dos veces al año)

Práctica 14 Pronunciation of 'h'

The letter 'h' is never pronounced in Spanish, except when preceded by 'c', when the letter combination is pronounced /tʃ/ as in English 'church'.

Ejercicio 58

Listen to the following words and repeat after the tone. Remember that the Spanish letter 'h' is silent.

hay, hermanito, hasta, ahora

Práctica 15 Intonation pattern of yes/no questions

Yes/no questions are interrogative sentences, the intonation of which rises on the first stressed syllable and is sustained until the last stressed syllable, where it rises again.

Ejemplo

¿Tú haces algo para conservar el medio ambiente?

Ejercicio 59

Listen to the questions and follow the intonation pattern by shadow reading them.

¿Y ustedes en la casa hacen algo de eso de reciclar?

¿A ti te gustaría tener un hermanito?

¿Entonces cambió tu opinión?

¿Sabes ya algo de los resultados del hospital?

In Spanish the difference between statements and yes/no questions is often only marked by the intonation. The statement *Zacarías se mete en la piscina* can be converted to the question *¿Zacarías se mete en la piscina?* by changing the pitch from falling at the end of the sentence to rising.

Cinta 1 Cara B

Ejercicio 60 | Convert the following statements to yes/no questions by changing the intonation as in the example.

> **Ejemplo**
>
> Zacarías tiene frío.   ¿Zacarías tiene frío?

Isabel quiere un té de canela.

Allariz es Patrimonio de la Humanidad.

Fuiste a la montaña de vacaciones.

Ejercicio 61 | Make the following statements into yes/no questions after the tone, following the example. Note that the statements in the first person need to be changed to the *usted* form.

> **Ejemplo**
>
> Le voy a tratar el resfriado con aspirina.
>
> ¿Me va a tratar el resfriado con aspirina?

Tomo manzanilla para la indigestión.

Hace el té de canela con agua.

Reciclo en casa por conveniencia.

Los clientes llegan el fin de semana.

Práctica 16 Pronunciation of words that change meaning with shifts in stress

Stress can be used in Spanish to distinguish between words of different meaning or function. If the stress changes, so can the meaning, for example: *critico* and *criticó*.

Ejercicio 62 | Listen to the following pairs of words and notice how stress changes their meaning.

rescate (a) rescue, ransom	*rescaté* I rescued
callo callus	*cayó* fell
critico criticize	*criticó* criticized
río river	*rió* laughed

Ejercicio 63

Listen to the following words and after the tone give a second word with the same spelling but with the stress on the other syllable, as in the example.

> **Ejemplo**
>
> guiso   guisó

salto I jump

canto I sing

lleno I fill

Ejercicio 64

Listen to the following words which have three different meanings, depending on where the stress falls, and repeat.

término termino terminó

árbitro arbitro arbitró

capítulo capitulo capituló

Do you know what each word means? (Look in the *Clave*.)

Ejercicio 65

Write down the sentences on the cassette as you hear them. If necessary, stop the cassette.

Práctica 17 The sound /rr/

In *Práctica 5* you learned that the sound /r/ is pronounced with a single flap of the tongue against the upper tooth ridge as in US English 'da**dd**y', 'pre**tt**y' or 'be**tt**er'. For the sound /rr/ the tongue adopts the same position, but it repeats the flaps (usually three times), very much like the rolled 'r' of some Scottish dialects.

The letter 'r' is pronounced /rr/ at the beginning of a word.

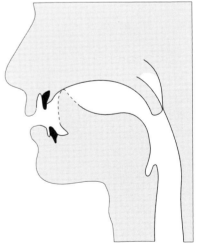

Articulación de [rr]

Ejercicio 66 | Listen to the words and repeat after the tone.

Rivera, república, represión, reforma

The /rr/ sound also occurs after 'n', 'l', or 's', where it is represented in written Spanish by the letter 'r'.

Ejercicio 67 | Listen to the words and repeat after the tone.

Enrique, alrededor, Israel, sonrisa

When the sound /rr/ occurs in intervocalic position (i.e. between two vowels), it is represented by the letter 'rr'.

Ejercicio 68 | Listen to the following words and repeat after the tone.

correspondió, morriña, tierra, territorio

There are pairs of words which differ in meaning, where the only difference in spelling and pronunciation is 'rr' /rr/ or 'r' /r/.

Ejercicio 69 | Read the following pairs of words or expressions and notice the difference in meaning. Then listen to the cassette and repeat after the tone.

poro pore	*porro* porro (type of dance)
enterado informed	*enterrado* buried
¡sin peros! no buts!	*¡sin perros!* no dogs!
foro forum	*forro* cover

Ejercicio 70 | Listen to the following tongue-twister in full, then rewind the cassette and repeat it line by line after the tone. Finally read it aloud.

Erre con erre cigarro,
Erre con erre barril,
Rápido ruedan los carros
Cargados de azúcar al ferrocarril.

Cinta 2 Cara A

31

Práctica 18 Pronunciation of the letter 'ñ'

The sound represented in written Spanish by the letter 'ñ' is pronounced with the tip of the tongue against the back of the lower teeth and the tongue pressed against the palate. It is the sound represented by the 'gn' of the word 'lasagne' or the 'ni' of the word 'onion'.

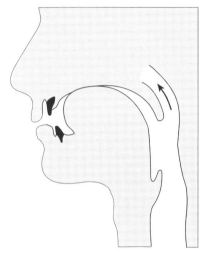

Articulación de [ɲ]

Ejercicio 71

Listen to the following words and repeat after the tone.

acompañar, español, año, morriña

There are pairs of words which differ in meaning, where the only difference in spelling and pronunciation is 'ñ' [ɲ] or 'n' [n].

Ejercicio 72

Read the following pairs of words and notice the difference in meaning. Then listen to the cassette and repeat after the tone.

Toño Tony	*tono* tone
baño bath, toilet	*vano* vain
cañas canes	*canas* white hair
sueña dreams	*suena* sounds

/ɲ/ and /ni/ sound similar to the Anglophone ear, but must be pronounced and understood as different sounds.

Ejercicio 73 | Listen to the following pairs of words and expressions and repeat after the tone. Notice the difference in meaning.

uñón big finger nail   *unión* union

aliñar to season   *alinear* to line up

huraño shy, unsociable   *uranio* uranium

de moño with hair in a bun *demonio* demon

Ejercicio 74 | Listen to the pronunciation of 'ñ' in the following nonsense rhyme, first in full, then rewind the cassette and repeat each line after the tone.

> Toño retoño se fue para el caño
> a buscar madroños, a pegarse un baño,
> cuando un ermitaño, añorando sueño
> le enseñó una viña, dañada, sin dueño.

Ejercicio 75 | Listen to the following poem by the Colombian poet Elvira Lascarro Mendoza.

> Duérmete, mi niño, mi niño marino,
> te daré mañana un lucero lindo.
>
> Duérmete y la luna te vendrá a contar
> un cuento bordado de espuma de mar.
>
> Pues mi niño bello quiere ser marino,
> le daré un velero de plata y armiño;
>
> Las nubes por velas, semejando azahares;
> de turrón el barco que errará en los mares.
>
> Te guiarán las hadas rubias de los cuentos
> hasta islas rosadas, en alas del viento.
>
> Duérmete mi niño, mi niño marino,
> te daré mañana un barco de armiño.

(Osorio, Fanny, *Lección de poesía. Selección de poemas para niños*, 1972, p. 67)

Práctica 19 Pronunciation of the letter combination 'ch'

The letter combination 'ch' represents the sound /tʃ/ as in English 'church' and 'chocolate'. In Spanish this letter combination is always pronounced /tʃ/, except in some dialects in Andalusia and in Caribbean Spanish, where it is often pronounced /ʃ/ as in English 'she'.

Cinta 2 Cara A

Ejercicio 76 | Listen to the following words and repeat after the tone.

Chapultepec, archivo, derecho, quechua

Ejercicio 77 | Read the following pairs of words and notice the difference between /tʃ/ and /k/. Then listen to the cassette and repeat after the tone.

charro Mexican cowboy	*carro* cart (Spain), car (Spanish America)
China China	*quina* cinchona bark
chorro jet of water	*corro* (I) run
Che	*que*

Ejercicio 78 | Listen for the pronunciation of /tʃ/ in the following proverbs; rewind the cassette and repeat each proverb.

Chocolate frío, échalo al río.

El chisme agrada, pero el chismoso enfada.

A la leche, nada le eches.

Ejercicio 79 | Listen for the pronunciation of /tʃ/ in the following tongue-twister, then rewind the cassette and repeat each line.

Un chavo dicharachero,
un charro con un chichón,
cachivaches y chicharras,
chile, chicha y chicharrón.

Práctica 20 Intonation patterns of content questions

Content questions are interrogative sentences which start with words like *qué, quién, cómo, dónde, cuándo, por qué, para qué,* etc. They have an intonation contour which falls at the end of the question and a higher starting pitch than that of a statement.

Listen to the following question:

¿Quiénes se casaron la semana pasada?

This shows that the question starts with a raised pitch on the word *quiénes,* followed by a slight fall in pitch which is sustained all the way to the word *pasada,* where it falls below the normal level.

Ejercicio 80	Listen to the following questions and notice the intonation pattern and the places where the pitch changes. Then repeat the questions after the tone. (Rewind the cassette if necessary.)

> ¿Quién fue César Vallejo?
>
> ¿Cómo vinieron vestidos los novios?
>
> ¿En qué consistió el rito del matrimonio?
>
> ¿Qué pasó luego?

Ejercicio 81	Listen to the following statements and convert them into questions, using the question word given as in the example. Say the complete question after the tone.

> ### Ejemplo
>
> _____ ese día se hace... (¿Qué?)   ¿Qué se hace ese día?
>
> _____ se celebra (¿Cuándo?)
>
> _____ pasa ese día (¿Qué?)
>
> _____ llevas celebrando el carnaval (¿Cuánto tiempo?)

Ejercicio 82	Here are a few more questions for you to practise. Read each question aloud after the tone.

– ¿Cuál es tu trabajo?

– ¿Qué es un balneario?

– ¿Para qué viene la gente aquí?

– ¿Para qué son beneficiosas las aguas del balneario?

This intonation pattern changes when the speaker expresses disbelief, surprise, anger, etc. or when an answer to a previous question was not fully understood. In this case, the pitch rises at the end of a question.

> – Tengo 110 años.
>
> – ¿Cuántos años tiene?

Ejercicio 83	React to the following statements by asking questions in a way that shows surprise, anger, amazement, curiosity, etc. Use the question words or expressions given.

> Mi trabajo es masajista de ovejas.   (¿Cuál?)
> ¿Cuál es su trabajo?

Aquí venía Picasso cada fin de semana.   (¿Quién?)

Viene gente de más de cien años.   (¿Qué clase?)

Las aguas son buenas para el libido.   (¿Para qué?)

Práctica 21 Vowels in contact: two-vowel synalepha

When a word ending in a vowel is followed by a word beginning with a vowel, the two vowels are pronounced as a single syllable; this is called 'synalepha'. For instance, in the sentence *En el Palacio Nacional se encuentran los murales que muestran la historia de México*, the sequence *se encuentran* is pronounced as /sen'kuentran/ and *la historia* as /lais'toria/. Where the vowels are the same (as in *se encuentran*), they merge into one vowel; where they are different (as in *la historia*), they form a diphthong.

Synalepha is a normal, common phenomenon of Spanish speech (even when speakers read out either aloud or in their heads), and it is not considered slovenly or careless use of the language. It always occurs, unless there is a pause for breath, hesitation or emphasis or when the speaker speaks very slowly.

Ejercicio 84

Listen to the following expressions where vowel assimilation occurs.

la abolición, clase explotada, mi hijo, sin embargo otros, su uniforme

Ejercicio 85

Listen to the following pairs of words and, after the tone, repeat them, forming the vowel assimilation, as in the example.

Ejemplo

a Almería

para asistir

mucha alegría

personaje español

Ejercicio 86

Listen to the following examples, in which vowels join up to form diphthongs across word boundaries.

aquí en España	casi una tragedia
la iglesia moderna	su abuelo murió

Cinta 2 Cara A

When the vowels in contact are not the same and do not constitute a diphthong (see *Práctica 4* for diphthong combinations), one of the vowels changes to form a diphthong. For instance, in *me avisa*, the /e/ of *me* becomes /i/ to form the diphthong /ia/ with the /a/ of **a**visa: /mia'bisa/.

Ejercicio 87

Listen to the following extract from *Como agua para chocolate,* a novel by the Mexican writer Laura Esquivel. Read it aloud afterwards.

> La cebolla tiene que estar firmemente picada. Les sugiero ponerse un pequeño trozo de cebolla en la mollera con el fin de evitar el molesto lagrimeo que se produce cuando uno la está cortando. Lo malo de llorar cuando uno pica cebolla no es el simple hecho de llorar, sino que a veces uno empieza, como quien dice, se pica, y ya no puede parar. No sé si a ustedes les ha pasado pero a mí la mera verdad sí. Infinidad de veces. Mamá decía que era porque yo soy igual… que Tita, mi tía abuela.

(Esquivel, Laura, *Como agua para chocolate, 1990,* p. 11)

Práctica 22 Pronunciation of 'l'

In Spanish, the sound /l/ is pronounced the same regardless of its position in a word. Whether at the beginning or at the end of a syllable, it is pronounced like in English 'luck', not like in 'pole' or 'call'. This sound is articulated with the tip of the tongue approaching or touching the upper alveoli, not with the back of the tongue touching the velum (soft palate). The Spanish 'l' is therefore alveolar, not velar.

Ejercicio 88

Listen to the following words and repeat after the tone.

> Lima, luego, bacalao, ilusiones

Ejercicio 89

Listen to the following words and repeat after the tone.

> gol, azul, mil, cultura

Ejercicio 90

Remember that 'll' *(doble l)* in Spanish is not pronounced /l/. Listen to the following words and repeat after the tone.

> amarillo, pollo, lluvia, allí

Ejercicio 91

Read the pairs of words overleaf, which show the contrast between 'll' and 'l', and notice the difference in meaning. As mentioned in *Práctica 10*, 'll' is pronounced like the 'y' in English 'yes' or the 'J' in 'John'. Then listen to the cassette and repeat after the tone.

Cinta 2 Cara A

llevar to take, carry, wear	*levar* to raise (an anchor)
lloro crying	*loro* parrot
pollo chicken	*polo* (North, South) Pole
halla (he, she) finds	*ala* wing

Ejercicio 92

Listen to the following English words and give the Spanish for each one after the tone. All the Spanish words contain an 'l'.

salt

goal

thousand

he

Ejercicio 93

Listen for the pronunciation of 'l' in the following proverbs and repeat each proverb during the gap.

Más logran las lágrimas que la lengua.

Flor de olivera en abril, aceite para el candil.

Real sobre real, principio es de caudal.

Look up their meaning in the *Clave*.

Práctica 23 Stress in single words: 'esdrújulas' and 'sobresdrújulas'

Remember that Spanish words with the stress on the third syllable from the end – *esdrújulas* – and with the stress on the fourth syllable from the end – *sobresdrújulas* – always have a written accent (*tilde*) on the stressed vowel e.g. *política, último, cómpramelo, corrígeselo*.

Ejercicio 94

Listen to the following words and repeat after the tone.

década, económico, tecnológico, Hispanoamérica

Ejercicio 95

Listen to the following sentences and repeat after the tone.

La informática es muy tecnológica.

Lo mínimo de lo económico es lo máximo.

En Hispanoamérica se dice 'chévere'.

A Cándido le gustan muchísimo las esdrújulas.

Ejercicio 96 | Listen to the following rhyme by the Colombian poet, Rafael Pombo, in full; then rewind the cassette and repeat it line by line. You can then read it aloud.

> Según díceres públicos doña Pánfaga hallábase hidrópica
> pudiera ser víctima de apoplético golpe fatal;
> su exorbitante estómago era el más alarmante espectáculo,
> fenómeno volcánico su incesante jadear y bufar.

(Pombo, Rafael, *Poesías completas,* 1957, p. 1145)

Ejercicio 97 | Listen to the following words and repeat after the tone.

> repítemelo, escúchatelo, sácatelos, escríbemelas

Práctica 24 Hiatos

In *Práctica 4* we looked at diphthongs, which are formed when two vowels, one of which is 'i' or 'u', come next to each other and form a single syllable. There are circumstances when the two vowels do not form a single syllable; this is indicated with a written accent, e.g. *solía, veníamos, compañía.* These vowel combinations are called *hiatos.*

Ejercicio 98 | Listen to the following words and repeat after the tone.

> tenía, querías, carpintería, estío

Ejercicio 99 | Complete each sentence with one of the words given, as in the example.

Ejemplo

El jardín _____ seis metros de largo.   (media, medía)

El jardín **medía** seis metros de largo.

Cada uno se comió _____ naranja.   (media, medía)

La _____ no es muy clara.   (ley, leí)

Yo no _____ esa carta.   (ley, leí)

Práctica 25 Loss of stress in single phonic groups

In Spanish, the following types of words lose their stress when accompanied by other words:

- the definite articles (*el, la, los, las, lo*);
- the possessive adjectives (*mi, tu, su, nuestro(s), -a(s), vuestro(s), -a(s)*);
- the object pronouns (*me, te, lo, la, le, se, nos, os, los, las, les*);

Cinta 2 Cara A

39

- the prepositions (except *según*);
- the relative pronouns (*que, quien(es), como, cual(es), cuando, donde*);
- the conjunctions *(y, o, pero, aunque*, etc.).

The stress falls on the word that follows. For example, *la biomasa* /labio'masa/, *mi abuela* /mia'βuela/, *a todos* /a'toδos/, *de conducta* /dekon'dukta/, *lo tuvo* /lo'tuβo/.

Ejercicio 100	Listen to the definite articles, object pronoun and possessive pronouns in isolation and then in combination with nouns and verbs. Listen for the difference in stress.

el	el cangrejo	lo	lo principal
tu	tu tierra	las	las encontré

Ejercicio 101	The indefinite articles and subject pronouns do not lose their stress. Listen to the contrast.

unos sistemas	los sis**te**mas
ellos vendían	los ven**dí**an
ellos contaban	nos con**ta**ban
tú hablabas	les ha**bla**bas

Ejercicio 102	Listen for the loss of stress in a poem by the Nicaraguan poet, Rubén Darío. Listen to the whole poem once and then shadow read it.

Sonatina

La princesa está triste… ¿qué tendrá la princesa?
Los suspiros se escapan de su boca de fresa,
que ha perdido la risa, que ha perdido el color.
La princesa está pálida en su silla de oro,
está mudo el teclado de su clave sonoro
y en un vaso, olvidada, se desmaya una flor.

El jardín puebla el triunfo de los pavos reales.
Parlanchina, la dueña, dice cosas banales,
y vestido de rojo, piruetea el bufón.
La princesa no ríe, la princesa no siente;
la princesa persigue por el cielo de Oriente
la libélula vaga de una vaga ilusión.

La princesa está triste… ¿qué tendrá la princesa?

(*Los 25.000 mejores versos de la lengua castellana*, 1969, pp. 364–5)

Práctica 26 [δ] and [r] in intervocalic position

In *Práctica 6* you came across the pronunciation of the letter 'd'. Remember that the most common pronunciation of this letter is [δ], which is pronounced like the 'th' of English 'that' and occurs in intervocalic position, whether within a word or across word boundaries.

Ejercicio 103

Listen to the following words and expressions containing the sound [δ] and repeat after the tone.

cambiado, la demora, ha sido todo, muy digno

The sound [δ] is often weakened to the point of disappearing. This is very common in normal speech, especially with the past participle ending in '-ado'. This shortening is not considered uneducated or careless speech.

The final 'd' of the positive familiar imperative *vosotros, -as* form is often replaced by an /r/ sound by some speakers in mainland Spain and the Canary Islands, for example *venir* rather than *venid* or *tomar* rather than *tomad*.

Ejercicio 104

Listen to the following sentences and expressions containing imperative forms.

¡Venid!, ¡Salid todos!, ¡Escuchad esto!, ¡Comed despacio!

Ejercicio 105

Read the following pairs of words where [r] and [δ] are contrasted and notice the difference in meaning. Then listen to the cassette and repeat after the tone.

mora blackberry	*moda* fashion
loro parrot	*lodo* mud
coro choir	*codo* elbow
toro bull	*todo* all

Ejercicio 106

Listen to the following sentences and for each one, decide which sound is being pronounced by saying *uno* for [r] or *dos* for [δ]. The answers are on the cassette.

Lo sé todo.

Eso ya no está de moda.

No canto en un coro.

¡No hay moros en la costa!

Cinta 2 Cara B

Práctica 27 Intonation pattern of exclamations

Exclamations follow an intonation pattern similar to that of statements, except that the pitch rises on the first stressed syllable and falls at the end of the sentence. The other important difference is the volume, which is normally louder than that of a statement.

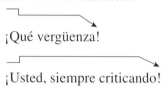

¡Qué vergüenza!

¡Usted, siempre criticando!

Ejercicio 107

Listen to the following exclamations. Pay attention to the intonation and the volume.

¡Voy, voy!

¡Pero todavía no me han enterrado!

¡Arrea, esto es una prueba de embarazo!

¡Rosita está de verdad embarazada!

Ejercicio 108

Listen to the following exclamations and repeat them after the tone.

¡Pero si es una niña todavía!

¡Y no está casada!

¡Menos mal que tú no estás aquí!

¡Embarazada a los dieciocho años!

Ejercicio 109

Listen to the following statements and convert them to exclamations after the tone as in the example.

Ejemplo
Toma esto y mira qué broma.
¡Toma esto y mira qué broma!

Esto es el colmo.

Pero si es verdad.

Isabel.

Práctica 28 Intonation pattern of multiple phonic groups: enumerations

Sentences with more than one pause are said to be composed of multiple phonic groups. For instance, in the sentence *En ella aparecen animales que hablan, cantan y bailan* there are three such phonic groups:

'En ella aparecen animales que hablan'; *'cantan'*; and *'y bailan'*.

In this example, the pitch falls at the end of each phonic group in the same way as for a statement, but rises and falls in the last phonic group.

Ejemplo

En ella aparecen animales que hablan, cantan y bailan.

Ejercicio 110

Listen for the intonation pattern in the following sentences and repeat after the tone.

– Los artistas espontáneos llenan el centro de Barcelona de música y de color.

– Es una película de melodrama y suspenso.

– Tengo una colección de postales de México, Argentina y Colombia.

aymará can also be spelt *aimara*.

– Puedo hablar español, quechua y aymará.

When the enumeration precedes the verb, the intonation rises on the last element of the enumeration.

Ejemplo

Los chistes, las historias y las canciones me encantan.

Ejercicio 111

Listen to the following sentences and repeat after the tone, as in the example.

– Los mimos, los payasos y los músicos animan el ambiente.

– La ópera, la música clásica y el jazz me gustan muchísimo.

– Los arlequines y las esculturas humanas son muy interesantes.

When the last element of the enumeration is not preceded by the conjunction *y*, the pattern is different. In this case, the intonation does not rise in the last group.

Ejemplo

Lo que más les gusta a los niños es la música, los animales.

Ejercicio 112

Listen to the following sentences and repeat after the tone.

– Es joven, tiene energía, con capacidad, es inteligente, sabe lo que quiere.

– Yo creo que a todos los niveles ha sido fantástico, me ha gustado mucho.

– Se ve una obra serena, madura.

Práctica 29 Stress in compound nouns

Compound nouns in Spanish can be formed by different methods, but by far the most common is the merging of a verb and a noun. The word *botafumeiro* is used to describe the giant incense burner inside the Cathedral of Santiago de Compostela. *Botafumeiro* is a compound noun formed by joining *bota* (from *botar*, to throw, spread) and *fumeiro*, a Galician word meaning 'incense'. Most typically, Spanish compound nouns are composed of a verb in the third person singular and a noun in the plural e.g. *lavaplatos: lava* (from *lavar*, to wash and *platos*, dishes). These compound words lose the stress on the verb and carry only the stress on the noun part: [laβa'platos].

Ejercicio 113

Listen to the following compound nouns, and repeat after the tone.

trotamundos, aguafiestas, pasamanos, cuentagotas

Práctica 30 Combinations of consonants

Consonantal clusters in Spanish are formed by the combination of 'p', 'b', 'f', 'g' and 'c' with 'l' and 'r', and 'd' and 't' with 'r' in the same syllable, resulting in the following combinations: 'pr', 'br', 'pl', 'bl', 'fr', 'fl', 'gr', 'gl', 'cr', 'cl', 'dr', 'tr': *profesión, abre, plato, retablo, fragancia, flor, gracias, glacial, cristal, claro, drama, trabajar.*

Ejercicio 114

Listen to the following sentences and repeat after the tone.

– El año pasado descubrí la artesanía de cristal.

– Estoy trabajando en una vinagrera.

– Alberto de León explica su complicada creación.

– Estamos representando la creación.

Ejercicio 115

Listen to the following passage from *La otra costilla de la muerte* by the Colombian writer and Nobel Prize winner, Gabriel García Márquez. Listen for consonantal clusters, underline them and then read the passage aloud.

Sin saber por qué, despertó sobresaltado. Un acre olor a violeta y a formaldehído venía, robusto y ancho, desde la otra habitación, a confundirse con el aroma de flores recién abiertas que mandaba el jardín amaneciente. Trató de serenarse, de recobrar ese ánimo que bruscamente había perdido en el sueño. Debía ser ya la madrugada, porque afuera, en el huerto, había empezado a cantar el chorro entre las legumbres y el cielo era azul por la ventana abierta. Repasó la sombría habitación, tratando de explicarse aquel despertar brusco, esperado. Tenía la impresión, la certidumbre física de que alguien había entrado mientras él dormía.

(García Márquez, Gabriel, extracto de *La otra costilla de la muerte*, en *Todos los cuentos*, p. 14)

Práctica 31 Assimilation of consonants

Consonant assimilation is not as common in Spanish as in English because Spanish words end in a very small number of consonants, namely 'd', 'j', 'l', 'm', 'n', 'r', 's' and 'z'. When one word ends and the next one begins with the same one of these letters, in normal speech assimilation occurs, resulting in the two consonants being pronounced as one. For example, ¿*Estás seguro?* is pronounced /es'taseguro/, with the final 's' of *estás* and the 's' of *seguro* merging into a single 's'.

Ejercicio 116

Listen to each of the following pairs of words said separately. Then pronounce them together after the tone.

> más sillas, red directa, son nuevos, el lago

Ejercicio 117

Listen to the following sentences and repeat after the tone.

El teatro infantil lo fundó un amigo.

Los animales se divierten.

No compran nada.

¿Es seguro?

Práctica 32 Pronunciation of words with two stresses: adverbs ending in '-mente'

Adverbs ending in '-mente' carry two stresses: one on the adjective or adverb they are derived from, and a second one on the first syllable of '-mente'. For example, the word *seguramente* is pronounced /se'gura'mente/.

Ejercicio 118 | Listen to the following words and repeat after the tone.

desesperadamente, realmente, mundialmente, completamente

Ejercicio 119 | For each of the following adverbs and adjectives give the corresponding adverb ending in '-mente'.

efectivo, terrible, último, desesperado

Ejercicio 120 | Listen to the following sentences and repeat after the tone.

El político se volvió completamente loco.

Esta maleta huele terriblemente mal.

El ruido cambiaba constantemente.

Nos sentimos completamente engañados.

Práctica 33 Pronunciation of 'x'

The letter 'x' is normally pronounced /ks/, except in a few words like *México* /'mehiko/, *Oaxaca* /ua'haka/ and others mostly derived from Aztec roots. It is never pronounced /gz/ as in English 'exam' or 'exit'.

Ejercicio 121 | Listen to the following words and repeat after the tone.

extremo, texto, existir, flexible

In normal speech, however, /ks/ is simplified to /s/ when 'x' precedes a consonant.

Ejercicio 122 | Listen to the following words and repeat after the tone.

pretexto, expulsar, contexto, Extremadura

Práctica 34 Intonation pattern of imperative sentences

Imperative sentences follow an intonation pattern similar to that of exclamations, with the pitch rising on the first stressed syllable and falling at the end of the sentence. In fact, many imperative sentences are exclamations.

As with exclamations, the voice volume is normally louder than that of a statement. Listen to the following examples:

¡Toma el poema!

¡Abre la puerta!

Ejercicio 123

Listen to the following exclamations. Pay attention to the intonation and the voice volume.

¡Contesta mis preguntas!

¡Dime que no es cierto!

¡Termina la carta!

Ejercicio 124

Listen to the following sentences and repeat after the tone.

¡Confiese la verdad!

¡Cállate!

Cálmense.

¡Déjame salir!

In the imperative negative, the main stress is on the word *no*.

Ejemplo

¡No te hagas el tonto!

Ejercicio 125

Listen to the following imperative sentences and convert them to the negative after the tone, as in the example.

Ejemplo

Traiga muchos regalos.   No traiga muchos regalos.

Abra la puerta.

Hablemos rápido.

Traigan muchas cosas.

Práctica 35 Intonation patterns of sentences with multiple phonic groups: parenthetic phrases

Parenthetic phrases are preceded and followed by short pauses. This is indicated in the written language by the use of commas, brackets or dashes. These phrases are normally said in a lower pitch of voice than the rest of the sentence and end in a rising pitch.

Por última vez – dijo Carlos – ¡cuéntame cuál es el problema!

Ejercicio 126

Listen to the following sentences and repeat after the tone.

¡Qué ingenua he sido! – pensó Isabel. No le perdonaré nunca.

Aquel nombre – Rosarito – significa mucho para Zacarías.

Su marido, que la ha seguido, no puede entrar.

Zacarías (con mucha afectación) recita el poema.

Práctica 36 Pronunciation of long words: verb forms with enclitics

Spanish imperatives, present participles and infinitives can have one or more pronouns attached to their ending. These pronouns are called enclitics or enclitic pronouns, e.g. *me* in *dime, la* in *viéndola* and *nos* in *lavarnos*. Often these combinations produce long words: *confiésalo, relajándose, descontaminarlas*.

Ejercicio 127

Listen to the following words and repeat after the tone.

dáselo, cálmate, dedicarlo, prestarme

Ejercicio 128

Listen to the following pairs of words and make up a longer word by adding the pronouns given, as in the example:

Ejemplo

entiende me   entiéndeme

confiesa lo   confiésalo

escribiendo se lo   escribiéndoselo

dedicar os lo   dedicároslo

adaptando se   adaptándose

buscando te   buscándote

Ejercicio 129   Listen to the following sentences, identify the long verbal forms with enclitics and say them aloud.

       Ejemplo

       ¿No quieres escribírmelo? Escribírmelo.

Isabel siempre está escribiéndoles.

¡Zacarías, déjanoslo ver!

Esa tarde Carlos decidió recomendárnoslo.

¡Rosita, cúbrete!

Práctica 37 Triphthongs and three-vowel synalepha

There are four triphthongs in Spanish: 'iai', 'iei', 'uai' and 'uei'. These groups of vowels are pronounced as one single syllable within a word, e.g. *estudiáis, limpiéis, situáis, actuéis*. They mostly occur in some verbal forms corresponding to *vosotros, -as*. These three-vowel combinations and many more are more common across word boundaries: *sí hay, su ahijado*.

Ejercicio 130   Listen to the following words and repeat after the tone.

       act**uái**s, b**uey,** no estud**iéi**s, limp**iái**s

Ejercicio 131   Listen to the following sentences and repeat after the tone.

       ¿Limp**iái**s las fichas todos los días?

       No me od**iéi**s sin motivo.

       ¿Cuándo camb**iái**s el horario?

       ¡No me env**iéi**s más mensajes!

Ejercicio 132   Listen to the following sentences and repeat after the tone.

       Noem**í e I**sabel salieron.

       Su aymará es perfecto.

       Fue Inés.

       Aqu**í ha e**stado siempre.

       Tú e Hilario deben ir.

Three-vowel synalepha is more common than triphthongs and gives rise to a large combination of vowels.

Ejercicio 133

Listen to and repeat the following sentences, where three vowels are pronounced as one.

Ana v**a a A**licante.

Josefa l**ee e**l periódico.

Juan**a ha a**ctuado bien.

No pel**ee e**n la calle.

Ejercicio 134

Listen to and repeat the following sentences, where three vowels are reduced to two.

Luisa v**a a U**ruguay.

En este rincón v**a a e**star mejor.

Juan**a ha o**cultado algo.

S**e ha** apuntado a una de sus actividades.

Práctica 38 Intonation pattern of disjunctive sentences

Disjunctive sentences have an intonation contour equivalent to that of a yes/no question followed by a statement, with a drop in pitch on the *o* or the *u*.

Esa Rosarito o como se llame.

Ejercicio 135

Join the following sentences and phrases with *o* to make up a disjunctive sentence.

Ejemplo

Margarita quiere estudiar alemán   (Francés).
Margarita quiere estudiar alemán o francés.

Zacarías escribe un poema   (Una carta de amor).

¿Rosita sale esta tarde?   (Esta noche).

¿Isabel le cree a Carlos?   (Al abuelo).

Práctica 39 Integrated activity

Ejercicio 136

Listen to the passage on the cassette without the transcript. Listen for the various sounds including /r/, /rr/, [δ], [β], the lack of aspiration in /p/, /t/ and /k/ and the clarity of the vowel sounds. Also, remember that the syllables are of roughly the same length and that there is no 'crunching' within words, even if they are long ones. Listen for stress in words.

Ejercicio 137

Listen to the passage again and now concentrate on word boundaries, especially those where synalepha occurs. Listen also for intonation patterns: questions, statements, enumerations and parenthetic phrases.

Ejercicio 138

Read the passage aloud at a comfortable speed; try all the cases of synalepha you have marked and the intonation patterns you have identified.

Ejercicio 139

Shadow read the passage, trying to keep pace with the recording.

> Platero es pequeño, peludo, suave; tan blando por fuera, que se diría todo de algodón, que no lleva huesos. Sólo los espejos de azabache de sus ojos son duros cual dos escarabajos de cristal negro.
>
> Lo dejo suelto, y se va al prado, y acaricia tibiamente con su hocico, rozándolas apenas, las florecillas rosas, celestes y gualdas… Lo llamo dulcemente: «¿Platero?», y viene a mí con un trotecillo alegre que parece que se ríe, en no sé qué cascabeleo ideal…
>
> Come cuando le doy. Le gustan las naranjas, mandarinas, las uvas moscateles, todas de ámbar, los higos morados, con su cristalina gotita de miel…
>
> Es tierno y mimoso igual que un niño, que una niña…; pero fuerte y seco por dentro, como de piedra. Cuando paseo sobre él, los domingos, por las últimas callejas del pueblo, los hombres del campo, vestidos de limpio y despaciosos, se quedan mirándolo:
>
> – Tien 'asero…,
>
> Tiene acero. Acero y plata de luna, al mismo tiempo.

(Jiménez, Juan Ramón, *Platero y yo*, 1980, p. 85)

Clave

Ejercicio 6
El melón.

Ejercicio 10
El viento.

Ejercicio 16
The diphthongs are shown in bold.

Empezamos d**ia**r**ia**mente a las s**ie**te tr**ei**nta recib**ie**ndo la g**ua**rd**ia** de las últimas v**ei**ntic**ua**tro horas. A las ocho pasamos a las salas a ver los pac**ie**ntes que han ingresado, eh… de una manera rápida. En una hora revisamos los ingresos. De las n**ue**ve a las once, paso visita en alguna de las salas específicas, eh… rotándolas. De once a doce tenemos alguna re**u**n**ió**n, algún tipo de ses**ió**n tamb**ié**n presentada por algún servic**io**. A las doce tenemos actividades… eh, del comité de calidad, o b**ie**n… eh, de actividad general del hospital. A partir de las dos de la tarde nos dedicamos a labores docentes, educativas hasta las catorce o… hasta las d**ie**cis**éi**s o d**ie**cis**ie**te horas.

Ejercicio 17
The diphthongs are in bold.

Nocturno
Padre n**ue**stro, que estás en los c**ie**los,
¿por qué te has olvidado de mí?
Te acordaste del fruto en febrero,
al llegarse su pulpa rubí.
¡Llevo ab**ie**rto tamb**ié**n mi costado
y no qu**ie**res mirar hac**ia** mí!

Me vend**ió** el que besó mi mejilla;
me negó por la túnica r**ui**n.

Yo **e**n mis versos el rostro con sangre,
como Tú sobre el paño, le di;
y **e**n mi noche del **Hue**rto me han sido,
Juan cobarde, y el Ángel hostil.

(*Los 25.000 mejores versos de la lengua castellana*, 1969, p. 391)

Ejercicio 21
estar   oír   salir   asir

Ejercicio 22
Prepararemos el material necesario.

Viajaremos en coche.

Nos comeremos una buena comida.

Ejercicio 30
jamón   juego   jarra   gente

Ejercicio 41
soy, ley, guay, estoy

Ejercicio 42
Hasta el cuarenta de mayo, no te quites el sayo.   Never cast a clout 'til May be out.

Mientras las armas hablan, las leyes callan.   While guns speak, the law is silent.

El asno chiquillo siempre es borriquillo.   A little donkey is always an ass.

Ejercicio 48
A tales tiempos, tales alientos.   Desperate times call for desperate measures. / Times change and we change with them.

Donde no hay mata, no hay patata.   If you don't plant the seed, you don't get the crop.

De tal palo, tal astilla.   A chip off the old block. / Like father, like son.

Ejercicio 61

¿Toma manzanilla para la indigestión?

¿Hace el té de canela con agua?

¿Recicla en casa por conveniencia?

¿Los clientes llegan el fin de semana?

Ejercicio 63

saltó jumped *cantó* sang

llenó filled

Ejercicio 64

término term *termino* I finish
terminó finished

árbitro referee *arbitro* I referee
arbitró refereed

capítulo chapter *capitulo* I capitulate
capituló capitulated

Ejercicio 65

Juan se **casó** el sábado pasado.

Paso a paso, Pedro **terminó** sus tareas.

Cuando **termino** mi trabajo, practico la natación.

Un préstamo a **término** fijo es muy práctico.

Ejercicio 78

Chocolate frío, échalo al río. Don't flog a dead horse.

El chisme agrada, pero el chismoso enfada. The gossip you enjoy, the gossip-monger annoys.

A la leche, nada le eches. Don't gild the lily.

Ejercicio 81

¿Cuándo se celebra?

¿Qué pasa ese día?

¿Cuánto tiempo llevas celebrando el carnaval?

Ejercicio 83

¿Quién venía aquí cada fin de semana?

¿Qué clase de gente viene?

¿Para qué son buenas las aguas?

Ejercicio 92

sal gol mil él

Ejercicio 93

Más logran las lágrimas que la lengua. Tears speak louder than / achieve more than words.

Flor de olivera en abril, aceite para el candil. If the olive tree blossoms too early, the oil is only fit for use in lamps.

Real sobre real, principio es de caudal. Take care of the pennies and the pounds will take care of themselves.

Ejercicio 115

The consonantal clusters are in bold.

Sin saber por qué, despertó so**br**esaltado. Un a**cr**e olor a violeta y a formaldehído venía, robusto y ancho, desde la o**tr**a habitación, a confundirse con el aroma de **fl**ores recién abiertas que mandaba el jardín amaneciente. **Tr**ató de serenarse, de reco**br**ar ese ánimo que **br**uscamente había perdido en el sueño. Debía ser ya la ma**dr**ugada, porque afuera, en el huerto, había empezado a cantar el chorro entre las legum**br**es y el cielo era azul por la ventana abierta. Repasó la som**br**ía habitación, **tr**atando de explicarse aquel despertar **br**usco, esperado. Tenía la impresión, la certidum**br**e física de que alguien había en**tr**ado mien**tr**as él dormía.

(García Márquez, Gabriel, extracto de *La otra costilla de la muerte*, en *Todos los cuentos*, p. 14)

Acknowledgements

Grateful acknowledgement is made to the following sources for permission to reproduce material in this book:

Text

Pages 16–17 and 52: Mistral, G., 'Nocturno', *Los 25.000 mejores versos de la lengua castellana*, © Editorial Vergara, SA 1963; *page 18:* Jiménez, J. R., Lorca, F. G. and Alberti, R. 1997, 'Mariposa del aire', *Mi primer libro de poemas*, Anzos SA; *page 33:* Mendoza, E. L. 'Para dormir al niño que amaba el mar' in Osorio, F. 1972, *Lección de poesía*, Instituto Colombiano de Cultura, Bogatá; *page 40:* Darío, R. 'Sonatina', *Los 25.000 mejores versos de la lengua castellana*, © Editorial Vergara, SA 1963.

En rumbo

Pronunciation Practice Booklet

Cuadernillo de pronunciación

Improve your spoken Spanish with the *En rumbo* pronunciation activities!
This booklet and the accompanying audio cassettes support the four-part
intermediate Spanish course *En rumbo*, but can equally be used on their own.
The cassettes feature exercises intended to improve your speaking and
listening skills, with speakers from different regions of the Spanish-speaking
world to familiarize you with a variety of accents.

The *En rumbo* Pronunciation Practice Booklet accompanies:

En rumbo 1 ISBN 0 415 20324 4

En rumbo 2 ISBN 0 415 20325 2

En rumbo 3 ISBN 0 415 20326 0

En rumbo 4 ISBN 0 415 20327 9

En rumbo is part of the Open University Spanish programme.
A bordo, an introductory course to *En rumbo*, is also available.

ISBN 0 415 20332 5

The Open University

ISBN 0-415-20332-5

9 780415 203326